HURRICANES

BE AWARE AND PREPARE

by Renée Gray-Wilburn

Consultant:
Joseph M. Moran, PhD
Meteorology, Professor Emeritus
University of Wisconsin-Green Bay

CAPSTONE PRESS
a capstone imprint

A+ Books are published by Capstone Press,
1710 Roe Crest Drive, North Mankato, Minnesota 56003
www.capstonepub.com

Library of Congress Cataloging-in-Publication Data
Gray-Wilburn, Renée.
  Hurricanes : be aware and prepare / by Renée Gray-Wilburn ; editor, Jill Kalz.
      pages cm — (A+ books. Weather aware)
  Summary: "Describes how hurricanes form, their effects, and how people can prepare for them"—Provided by publisher.
  Includes index.
  Audience: K-3.
  ISBN 978-1-4765-9903-8 (library binding)
  ISBN 978-1-4765-9908-3 (eBook PDF)
1. Hurricanes—Juvenile literature. I. Kalz, Jill. II. Title.
  QC944.2.G73 2015
  551.55'2—dc23   2014006647

Editorial Credits
Jill Kalz, editor; Lori Bye, designer; Svetlana Zhurkin, media researcher; Tori Abraham, production specialist

Photo Credits
Getty Images: Burton McNeely, cover; NASA, 2 (middle left), 8 (inset), 11, 12–13; Newscom: EPA/Joe Marquette, 24, Zumapress/The Palm Beach Post/Lannis Waters, cover (inset), 23; Shutterstock: B747, 1, 21, bikeriderlondon, 2 (left), 5, borsvelka (background), back cover and throughout, forestpath, 18–19, Harvepino, 6–7, Leonard Zhukovsky, 3 (left and right), 16, 28–29, Lev Radin, 3 (middle left), 22, Natalia Pushchina, 15, Patricia Marroquin, 17, Pixsooz, 3 (middle right), 25, Robert Ranson, 2 (right), 14, Stacie Stauff Smith Photos, 26, Tad Denson, 27; U.S. Navy: Jim Brooks, 2 (middle right), 8–9, Mass Communication Specialist 1st Class R. Jason Brunson, 20

Note to Parents, Teachers, and Librarians
This Weather Aware book uses full color photographs and a nonfiction format to introduce the concept of hurricanes. *Hurricanes: Be Aware and Prepare* is designed to be read aloud to a pre-reader or to be read independently by an early reader. Photographs help listeners and early readers understand the text and concepts discussed. The book encourages further learning by including the following sections: Table of Contents, Critical Thinking Using the Common Core, Glossary, Read More, Internet Sites, and Index. Early readers may need assistance using these features.

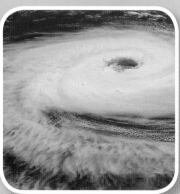

Printed in the United States of America in North Mankato, Minnesota
032014   008087CGF14

TABLE OF CONTENTS

BE WEATHER AWARE

Weather usually follows a pattern. But once in a while, the pattern changes. To keep yourself safe, be weather aware. Here you'll learn about hurricanes so you can better prepare for them.

WHAT IS A HURRICANE?

A hurricane is a powerful storm that forms over warm ocean water. Its winds are fast and strong. Hurricanes are also called typhoons or tropical cyclones. They can reach across hundreds of miles.

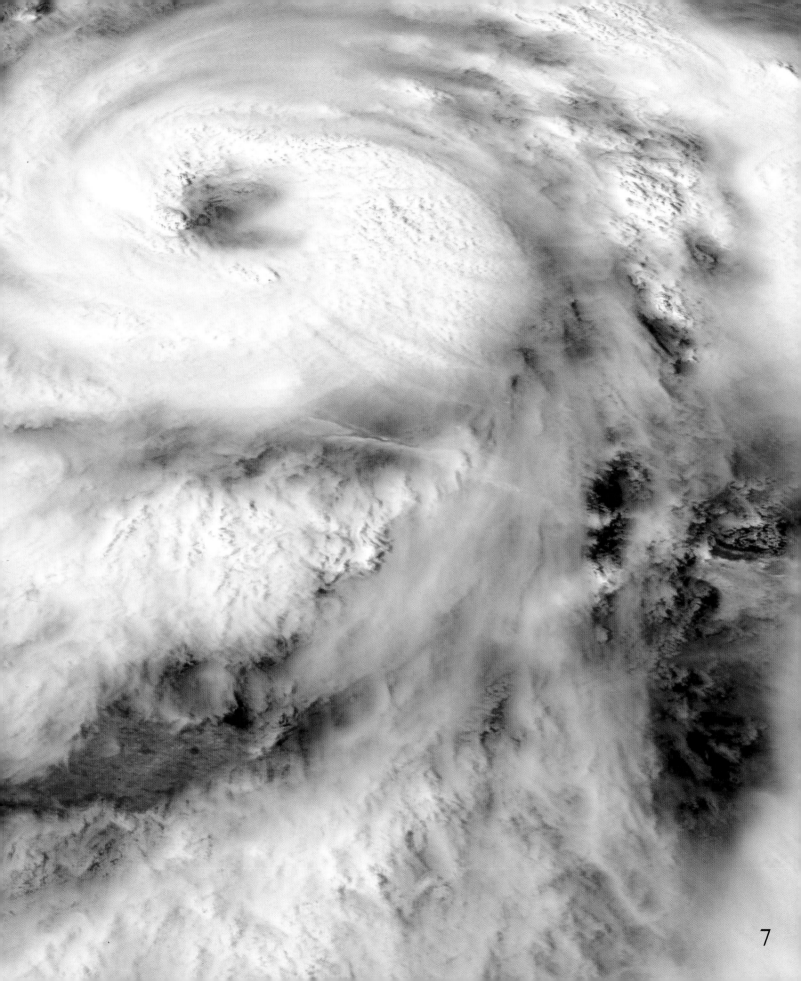

Viewed from above, hurricanes north of the equator spin counter-clockwise. Hurricanes south of the equator spin the opposite way.

Hurricane winds blow at least 74 miles (119 kilometers) per hour. Winds must stay above this speed for one minute or more to be called a hurricane.

Hurricane winds swirl around a center called the eye. Winds in the eye are nearly still. Skies are almost cloudless.

WHAT CAUSES HURRICANES?

Hurricanes form when warm ocean water evaporates. Water warmer than 80 degrees Fahrenheit (27 degrees Celsius) is best for hurricanes.

The warm water vapor rises. It then cools and condenses into storm clouds.

The rising air also creates wind.
The spinning of our planet makes the
wind swirl. The warmer the ocean
water, the faster the wind moves.

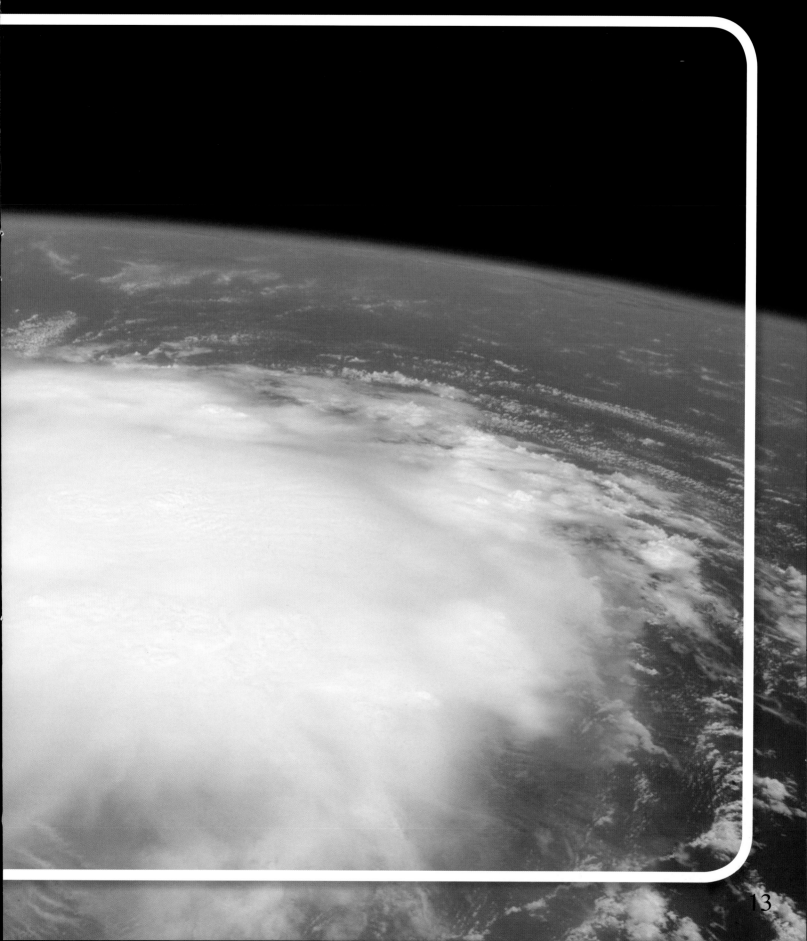

13

WHERE AND WHEN DO HURRICANES FORM?

Hurricanes form where ocean water is warmest. The warmest ocean water lies near the equator.

The surface waters of the Atlantic Ocean are warmest in late summer and early fall. The Atlantic hurricane season runs from June through November. The biggest danger to the United States is between mid-August and late October.

Hurricanes are named in ABC order, starting with the first hurricane of the season. In 2013 the first three hurricanes in the Atlantic Ocean were named Andrea, Barry, and Chantal.

WHY ARE HURRICANES DANGEROUS?

Hurricanes can cause much property damage. Their strong winds tear apart buildings and toss debris. Hurricanes may produce powerful tornadoes. They also bring heavy rain. The rain can cause flooding far from the coast.

Top 5 Costliest Hurricanes in U.S. History

$ $ $ $ $ $ 1. Katrina—2005, Gulf Coast (about $108 billion)

$ $ $ $ 2. Sandy—2012, New York/New Jersey (about $65 billion)

$ $ 3. Ike—2008, Texas (about $29.5 billion)

$ $ 4. Andrew—1992, Florida (about $26.5 billion)

$ 5. Wilma—2005, Florida (about $21 billion)

The worst hurricane damage often comes from a storm surge. When a hurricane reaches land, its winds push lots of water onto the shore. The storm surge can cause flooding. It can destroy shoreline roads and buildings.

Islands and places along coasts are hit hardest during a hurricane. But even areas far from the coast are in danger. Slow-moving hurricanes can cause wind, rain, and flooding for days or weeks.

PIZZA
WATER STREET
GOURMET
DELI
WATER STREET GOURMET
WATER STREET
GOURMET

HOW DO YOU PREPARE FOR A HURRICANE?

Meteorologists study where and when hurricanes may strike. They try to give people time to get ready. Some people prepare homes and businesses by nailing boards over windows. They bring inside anything that might blow around.

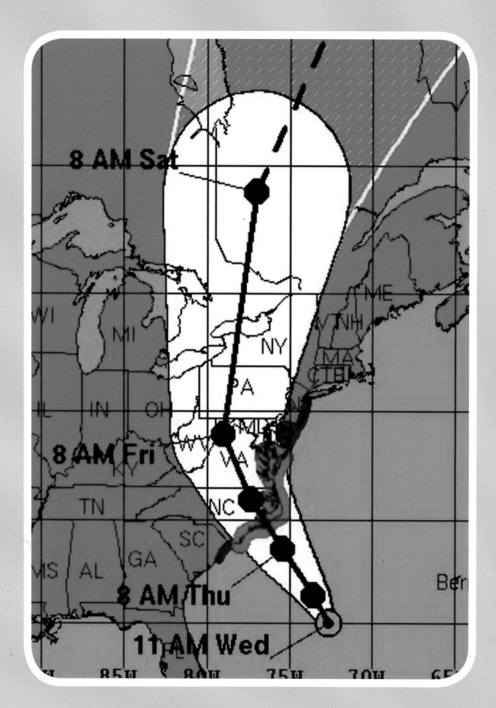

a map showing the likely path of a hurricane

You can prepare for a hurricane by making an emergency kit. Pack the kit with food and water that will last for at least three days. Include first-aid supplies, a flashlight, batteries, a weather radio, and a blanket.

EMERGENCY PREPARATION CHECKLIST

Section 1: Emergency Survival Items:

☐ Water Containers
☐ First Aid Kit
☐ Torch
☐ Battery Operated Radio
☐ Batteries
☐ Tinned Food (non-perishable)
☐ Can Opener
☐ Dust Masks

In an emergency you will
It is essential to gath
in case of an e

EVACUATION
ROUTE

3 21 06
LS

Sometimes, leaving the area until the storm has passed is the best choice. Plan an escape path. Learn which roads lead quickly away from the hurricane. Knowing where to go and what to do is the best way to stay safe.

While some hurricanes do cause lots of damage, most are not deadly. Hurricanes are simply a natural part of our world's weather. They can be scary. But they don't have to be, if you're weather aware.

CRITICAL THINKING USING THE COMMON CORE

1. Describe how, where, and when a hurricane forms. (Key Ideas and Details)

2. Describe how hurricanes can be dangerous. (Craft and Structure)

3. Explain the steps you would take at your home to prepare for a hurricane. (Integration of Knowledge and Ideas)

GLOSSARY

condense (kuhn-DENS)—to change from a gas to a liquid

debris (duh-BREE)—the scattered pieces of something that has been broken or destroyed

equator (i-KWAY-tuhr)—an imaginary line around the middle of Earth

evaporate (i-VA-puh-rayt)—to change from a liquid to a gas

meteorologist (mee-tee-ur-AWL-uh-jist)—a person who studies and predicts the weather

property (PROP-ur-tee)—a house, building, or land belonging to someone

storm surge (STORM SURJ)—a sudden, strong rush of water that happens as a hurricane moves onto land

water vapor (WAH-tur VAY-pur)—water in gas form

READ MORE

Aboff, Marcie. *Hurricanes!* Wild Earth. Mankato, Minn.: Capstone Press, 2012.

Adamson, Heather. *Surviving a Hurricane.* Be Prepared. Mankato, Minn.: Amicus, 2012.

Baltzer, Rochelle. *Hurricanes.* Natural Disasters. Edina, Minn.: ABDO Pub. Co., 2012.

Gibbons, Gail. *Hurricanes!* New York: Holiday House, 2009.

INTERNET SITES

FactHound offers a safe, fun way to find Internet sites related to this book. All of the sites on FactHound have been researched by our staff.

Here's all you do:

Visit *www.facthound.com*

Type in this code: 9781476599038

Check out projects, games and lots more at
www.capstonekids.com

INDEX